Encyclopædia Britannica

Fascinating Facts

How Things Work

PUBLICATIONS INTERNATIONAL, LTD.

Louis Weber, C.E.O.
Publications International, Ltd.
7373 North Cicero Avenue
Lincolnwood, Illinois 60646

Printed in USA.

8 7 6 5 4 3 2 1

ISBN: 1-56173-321-0

Staying in the Air

Airplanes stay in the air because their wings provide lift to hold them up. Airplane wings are flat on the bottom with an asymmetrical curve on top. Air moving over the upper surface of the wing has to travel faster and farther than air moving under the wing. This causes low pressure above the wing that sucks the wing upward and keeps the plane in the air.

Taking Off

The most difficult part of aircraft flight is actually getting the plane into the air. In order to lift itself up into the air, a plane must be moving forward very fast. This speed gets the air moving over the wings in such a way that it can lift the plane upward. Today's jumbo jets are so large that they must often use a runway 10,000 feet (3000 m) long in order to get enough lift to go up into the air. The power for getting down the runway and moving through the air comes from the plane's engines.

For the Adventuresome

Gliders stay in the air by going fast enough for the wings to give them the lift needed to stay in the air. The pilot simply keeps the glider pointed slightly downward so that the air under the wings pushes the glider upward as it heads back to the ground. Gliders are easy to keep in the air because they are light in weight and have very long wings. Their weight and wings help them catch upcurrents of air, or "thermals."

Glider

Getting Gliders To Fly

The biggest problem in flying a glider is getting it into the air. Many gliders are towed into the air behind airplanes. Others are launched from behind fast-moving cars. Some gliders have even been shot into the air by giant rubber cords—like a slingshot shooting a rock or stick.

That's a Big Kite!

Hang glider

A modern hang glider is really very much like a kite. The airfoil, or wing, is made of cloth that has been stretched over a lightweight metal frame. The pilot hangs underneath in a special harness. In most cases, the pilot gets the hang glider into the air by running down a hillside. Once the glider is in the air, currents of warm air lift it and keep it soaring along. The pilot can steer the hang glider by moving the control bar. This moves the position of the airfoil and allows the hang glider to change directions.

Whirlybird Maneuvers ►

Helicopters use their whirling rotors to lift themselves from the ground. They can go up or down depending on how the rotors are angled. If the rotors are angled sharply up, for example, the helicopter will go up. By tilting the rotors one way or the other, a pilot can also make a helicopter go right or left.

Let's Go Fly a Kite ▲

All kites work in pretty much the same way. The body of the kite gives it enough lift to stay in the air. To get a kite up, start by unwinding a few feet of the flying cord. Then run into the wind until the kite lifts up into the air. Once the kite is in the air, stand with your back to the wind. Let out more cord whenever the wind carries the kite farther up into the air. Pull in the cord whenever the kite falls back toward the ground.

Balloons Afloat ▲

A helium balloon floats because it weighs less than the air it moves through, since helium is an extremely lightweight gas. It is lighter than the air around us. Therefore, when the balloon has been filled with helium, it can rise up and float through the air.

Riding in a Hot-air Balloon ▼

Giant, colorful, hot-air balloons are filled with hot air or helium gas. This makes the balloon and its passenger compartment lighter than the air around it, so the balloon rises up into the sky. In fact, a filled balloon wants to rise so much that it must be held down by heavy sandbags kept inside the passenger compartment. Ropes are also used to tie balloons to the ground until everyone is ready for liftoff. The pilots can make the balloons go higher by throwing sandbags out of the compartment. When they want to land, the pilots simply let air out of the balloon.

Boats Afloat

Boats float for the same reason that branches, leaves, or even light pieces of metal do not sink in the water. They float because they weigh less than the water that is pushed out of the way as they go along the surface. Boats are man-made objects that are light enough to do the same thing. This is why the first boats were dugout canoes—logs that were hollowed out to take away weight and to make room for people to sit. Later, reeds and lightweight wood were used. Today, steel and fiberglass are most often used, since these are both light in weight and strong enough to hold people and goods safely.

Catching the Wind

Sailing with triangular sails became popular when people realized that they could shift the sail from side to side in order to keep it filled with wind. This way, they could sail from place to place even if the wind was not blowing exactly in that direction.

Propeller Wonders▲

Propellers have blades coming out of a central hub. Each of these blades forms a spiral from the hub. When the propeller turns, air or water is pushed around and around and "thrust," as movement forward or backward is called, is produced. This pushes the boat or airplane. Turning the blades in the opposite direction can make a boat move backward. Airplanes, as you've probably noticed, do not really back up too often.

Steering a Sailboat

A boat's sails must be kept pointing either toward or away from the wind so that they stay filled with wind. The boat is actually steered with a piece of wood or metal called a "rudder." The rudder sticks out behind the boat and controls how the water moves past it. By moving the rudder to the left, for example, the boat will move to the right, and vice versa.

Amazing Boomerangs

You probably will be surprised to learn that not all boomerangs come back to you. Some boomerangs are straight, not curved, and they are used as deadly hunting weapons. "Return" boomerangs are curved and have one flat side and one that is rounded.

Switching Gears

Gears are different-sized wheels that control how many times you must pedal in order to turn a bicycle's back wheel. If the bike's chain wheel (the wheel that the chain is on) were the same size as the wheel it was attached to at the back of the bike, the rear wheel would turn around once each time your pedals went around. If that chain wheel were twice as big, the rear wheel would go around twice each time your pedals turned. By having the bicycle chain work wheels of different sizes, you can make it easier to pedal when you are going up a hill and give yourself more pedaling power when you are cruising along a flat road or rushing down a hill.

It's as Easy as Riding a Bike

Today's bicycles are made of a metal—usually steel or aluminum—frame between two wheels of the same size. When the rider pushes down on the bike's pedals, the crank (the long piece of metal that the pedals are mounted to) turns the chain wheel and chain. The chain is connected to the rear wheel so that the rear wheel turns as you pedal. This pushes the bike forward. The only problem then is keeping your balance!

Putting on the Brakes

Two main types of brakes are used on bicycles today. The more old-fashioned kinds of brakes are made of pieces of metal that press against the hub (the center part) of a bike's rear wheel. Pressing backwards on your pedals makes the brake push against the hub. If you press lightly, the wheel turns slower. If you press hard, the wheel stops completely. Hand or "caliper" brakes are found on racing and mountain bikes. These have small levers that press pieces of rubber against the sides (the rims) of the front and back wheels. Again, the harder you press the slower the wheel is going to turn.

Boomerang Techniques

Skilled boomerang throwers like the aborigines of Australia can make boomerangs travel over 100 feet (30 m) in a straight line and then turn around in a 160 foot (50 m) circle before returning to them. They can even make boomerangs hit the ground, circle in the air, and then return.

A Man-made Fish

A submarine dives under the ocean by filling its tanks with water. Once underwater, it can float just like a fish, using its propellers to push itself forward, backward, and to the sides. To bring the submarine to the surface, the crew puts compressed air into the tanks. This forces the water out, making the ship lighter and bringing it to the surface.

Violin Music

Violin strings are stretched across a long, thin piece of wood called the "fingerboard." Attached to this is the belly, or soundbody, of the instrument, which makes the sound of the strings louder. Instead of plucking on the strings (the way you do with a rubber band or a guitar), a violinist scrapes a bow back and forth over the strings. This makes the basic sound of the violin. The sounds can be changed by pressing down on the strings with your fingers to make them shorter or longer—this makes the sounds higher or lower in pitch. By scraping the bow across more than one string at a time, the violinist can play chords, or more than one note at a time.

Playing a Guitar

Guitar players make music by plucking the strings that stretch along the instrument's fingerboard and body. On a regular, or acoustic guitar, the body is designed to increase the sound so that it can be heard by everyone. Electric guitars, on the other hand, use electricity to increase the sound made by plucking the strings. The notes are then reproduced through loudspeakers—which is where the sound comes from when someone plays an electric guitar.

Let's Play the Piano

Despite the way a piano looks, piano music actually comes from strings. Inside a piano are dozens of strings, not very different from the ones you see on a guitar or violin. The length of each string gives it its pitch—high, low, and so on. Pressing up against each string is a "damper," a piece that rests against the string and keeps it from vibrating and making any sound. When you press down on one of the piano's keys, the damper moves away from the string. Then, a small hammer strikes the string and makes the sound. The space inside the piano increases the sound so that it can be heard all over a large room.

From Grapes to Raisins

Raisins are actually dried grapes, which are made in several different ways. Natural raisins are dried in the sun until they turn a grayish-black color. Golden bleached raisins are treated in a special liquid, then exposed to fumes from burning sulfur, and finally dried in a tunnel that slowly takes the water from them. Each of the other different types of raisins is made in pretty much the same ways.

Popping Popcorn

Popcorn pops because it has smaller, harder kernels than other corn. It also has an outer shell that surrounds a lot of moist, starchy material. When the kernels are heated, the moisture inside them turns to steam. When the steam builds up enough pressure, it inflates the starch granules. This causes the kernels to burst and turns them inside out.

Our Favorite Dessert

Ice cream is made of milk fat, sugar, air, and flavors. (Some ice creams also use eggs, but most do not.) You begin by mixing together the milk fat and sugar. This mixture is then heated to kill any germs that might have collected. Then, it is mixed together once again to break the milk fat into tiny pieces. Next, it is stored at a freezing temperature for a while. Every once in a while, the ice cream is mixed to keep it smooth and to keep pieces of ice from getting into the mixture. Then, it is put back in the freezer. Flavors—vanilla, chocolate, fruit, whatever—are usually added while the ice cream is being mixed or frozen.

◄ Who Put the Holes in the Cheese?

All cheeses are made by separating the solid part, or curd, from the watery part of sour milk. Swiss cheese is made by taking the curd and heating it to around 125°F (52°C). Then, it is pressed into blocks or circles called "wheels." While the cheese is being stored, carbon dioxide gas (the same gas that we breathe out through our mouths) forms and makes the holes that have made Swiss cheese famous.

Why We Cook

When food is heated, chemicals inside of it change. This not only makes the food easier for our stomachs to work on, it also helps stop the action of germs that can cause disease. Cooking actually can use any one of a dozen methods—baking, boiling, or soaking the food in juices and chemicals that carry out the same chemical process as heating.

The History of Ovens

Long ago, people learned to cook by holding their food over a burning fire. Later, they found that they could make ovens out of stone or clay. These ovens were usually round and could be closed off from the outside in order to hold in the heat. By putting a hole in the oven to take out the smoke, people created an oven that cooked things slowly without burning. Heat either came from a fire underneath or from hot rocks placed inside the oven itself.

Cooking Made Easy

The first closed cooking stoves were invented at the end of the 1700s. These stoves let people control the amount of fire inside the oven better. By the 19th century, stoves were improved. They burned coal or gas and incorporated burners or hot plates, ovens, and boilers for heating water. In the 20th century, electric stoves became more commonplace.

A Cook's Best Friend

The food processor provides cooks with a handy machine for chopping, slicing, and mixing. In the base of the machine is a small electric motor. When the motor is turned on, it turns a shaft that sticks up inside the "work bowl," or the plastic bowl that holds the food. To chop food, the cook attaches two small blades that whirl around and cut the food into tiny pieces. These blades can also stir liquids and mix things that are already chopped up. To slice food, the cook attaches a sharp slicing blade against which the food is pressed to cut it into small pieces.

Baking pastries requires an oven.

9

The Story of Vinegar

Vinegar is made from wine in countries where wine is made, but it may also be made from malted barley, apples, sugar, or rice. Whatever alcoholic liquid is used is pumped into a vessel that is capable of holding up to 12,000 gallons (45,000 liters), although it is only half filled. In the middle of the vessel is a stage on which layers of birch twigs are placed, and below this air holes are bored in it. The liquid is then pumped over the birch twigs through a sparge, which is just like the sprinkler used for watering gardens. This way, a large amount of the liquid is exposed to the air. The process takes about six days; after this time, the vinegar is kept for some months in large storage vessels for the right flavor to be produced.

An Age-old Food

Yogurt is a food that originated in Turkey and the Balkan countries. When yogurt is produced commercially, skimmed milk powder is usually added first to thicken the milk, and bacteria called *Streptococcus thermophilus* are also added to give the correct consistency and flavor. The milk must be at a temperature of about 111°F (44°C) for the bacteria to work. When the milk has cooled to 40°F (5°C), they stop working, but by that time the milk has thickened.

Making Wine

When wine grapes are picked at the end of summer, they are crushed soon after they are picked. Their juice (called must) mixes with the wine yeast found in the grapes themselves and starts to ferment. The wine yeast works to change the sugar in the must into alcohol, although there are many ferments that may spoil the wine. The wine maker exposes the must to the air, since the wine yeast thrives on oxygen and the bad ferments do not. The temperature of fermenting grape juice is also controlled, since the wine yeast works best at 76°F (24°C). When fermentation stops (10-30 days), the juice is transferred to a large wooden vessel called a cask. Six or nine months later, the product is wine. The wine may be bottled at once or, if it is very good quality, it may be left to mature for some months in the cask.

◄Trampling Wine Grapes

Wine grapes are either crushed by treading them or by machine. If people trample the grapes with their feet, the weight is not great enough to crush the seeds and add bitterness to the juice. Grapes are still trodden in some parts of Spain and Portugal, but most are crushed by machines.

Spices and Herbs

Spices are parts of plants used to flavor food. Leaves used in the same way are usually known as herbs. Sometimes, the same plant produces both a spice and herb—for example, coriander and dill.

A Popular Flavor

Licorice is the product of the long, sweet root of a plant of the pea family. It is a perennial that grows to 3 to 5 feet (0.9 to 1.5 m) with pale blue, pealike flowers and leaves of 9 to 17 leaflets. Licorice roots are dug when the plants are three years old. When harvested, they are full of water and must be dried for six months to a year. The dried roots are then cut or sawed into pieces 6 to 12 inches (15 to 30 cm), sorted, and baled.

To prepare licorice, the roots are crushed and boiled, and the remaining liquid is evaporated. This leaves a paste or black stick licorice. Prepared licorice is used in medicines as a cough remedy, as a laxative, and to make some medicines taste better. As a flavoring, it is used in candy, chewing gum, and beverages.

Very Popular Candy

Chocolate comes from cocoa beans. The fat of the cocoa bean, known as cocoa butter, has rare properties. When it is mixed with the powder from the roasted cocoa bean and sugar, and then allowed to cool, it sets firmly and cleanly into a brittle solid. In 1828, a Dutchman named Van Houten first learned to separate the fat from the beans. Chocolate candy is now one of the most common and popular forms of modern confectionery.

Watching Bread Rise

In breadmaking, yeast plants are mixed with starch to form yeast cakes, which are combined with dough. The yeast acts on the starch in the flour, first producing glucose (a form of sugar) and then alcohol and carbon dioxide. The carbon dioxide gas causes the dough to swell or "rise." When the dough is kneaded, the bubbles of carbon dioxide are broken down. When the bread is baked, the heat expands the carbon dioxide, making the bread rise some more. Finally, the carbon dioxide, alcohol, and most of the water are driven off and light, soft bread is left.

Soaping Up

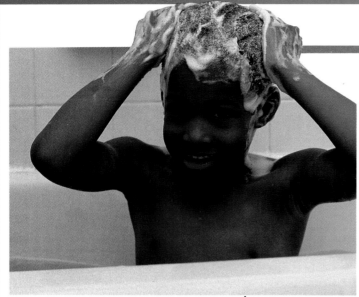

◀

Soap works to get rid of dirt because it attracts grease as well as water. Dirt is really a mixture of dirt particles and grease that sticks to clothing, skin, and just about anything else. It is also not soluble in water. When soap gets wet it forms a film. This film gets into the dirt and loosens the hold of the grease. Then, it wraps itself around the dirt, and the grease and dirt end up in the water around the soap.

Helping Someone to Breathe

Artificial respiration is a way to help people who have stopped breathing because of drowning, falling, or some other accident or illness. It is a method of breathing for another person until they can breathe on their own.

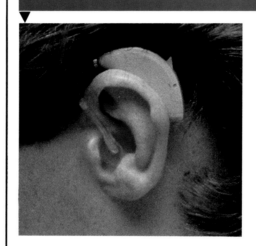

▼

Hearing a Pin Drop

Over the years, many different kinds of machines have been used to help people who have difficulty hearing. A hundred years ago, for example, people often used "ear trumpets," which were long tubes that made sounds louder. Today, however, hearing aids are usually electronic. They increase, or amplify, sounds the same way a microphone does. The most complicated kinds of hearing aids are bone-conduction aids, which are used by people whose outer and middle ears do not work at all. This kind of hearing aid makes vibrations that pass through to the person's inner ear. This allows them to hear almost as if their ears were perfectly healthy.

In Perfect Focus

"Farsighted" people cannot see things close to them. Their eyeball is too short or the lens of their eye is not the correct shape. Eyeglasses or contact lenses help these people by making sure that the light entering their eyes is bent at exactly the correct angle. This helps the eye focus on the light in the correct way.

A Crystal-clear World

Much of what "nearsighted" people see is blurred and unclear. Either their eyeball is too long from back to front or the lens of their eye is not the correct shape to bend the light rays coming into it. Eyeglasses or contact lenses help these people by bringing the light from distant objects to the correct point in their eyeball.

▶

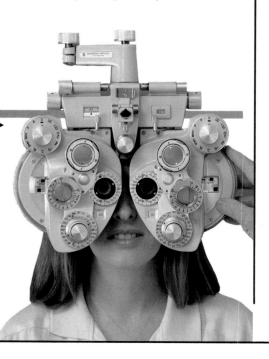

◄ Reading for the Blind

The Braille system for the blind uses raised dots to stand for each letter of the alphabet. One dot, for example, stands for the letter *A;* two dots, one on top of the other, for *B;* two dots side by side, for *C.* By feeling the dots of each letter, blind people can read everything from elevator signs to books.

Penicillin— The Wonder Drug!

For many years, penicillin was one of the most widely used medicines in the world because it was able to kill hundreds of different kinds of germs without harming patients. This wonder drug is actually an unusual mold that was discovered in the laboratory of Sir Alexander Fleming, a British doctor. This strange mold had the remarkable ability to stop the growth of bacteria, including those that caused such diseases as pneumonia, diphtheria, and sore throats.

Fixing Broken Bones ◄

A sharp blow, fall, or other injury can break almost any of your bones. Broken bones often heal easily. Doctors return the pieces of the bone to their normal position. Then they use a cast of some kind—plaster, plastic, or even air held inside a plastic bubble—to keep the bone from moving around. After a while, the bone begins to grow back together. Soon, the broken bone has healed. Strangely enough, bones that have been broken are often stronger than they were before, simply because the bone cells are newer and less worn.

Teeth for Eating

Humans have several different kinds of teeth that help us bite and chew our food. Of a person's 32 teeth, the first eight, in the front of the mouth, are incisors. These are used for cutting—pulling food apart, getting it off one surface or another, and so on. The next four teeth are the canines, which help rip food apart. Behind these are all the different kinds of molars—these are the grinding teeth. Food sits on the lower ones and is crushed as the upper and lower molars grind together. Although all of this sounds complicated—as if you had a whole factory in your mouth—you actually bite and chew without thinking. The entire process takes just a few seconds and almost no effort at all!

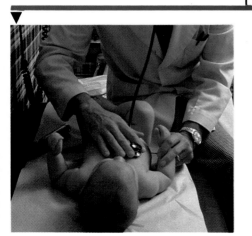

Hearing a Heartbeat

The stethoscope was invented in the early 1800s by a young French doctor, René Laennec. The idea for the invention came from watching children placing their heads to each other's chests in order to listen to heartbeats. Laennec took the idea further by using a perforated wooden cylinder. When he placed one end of the cylinder to a patient's chest and the other to his ear, he discovered that he could hear the patient's heartbeats much better.

A Painless Sleep ▶

Before major surgery, an injection in the arm puts the patient to sleep. The anesthesiologist then puts a mask on the patient's face through which he or she breathes in anesthetic gas, which is kept in special containers. The anesthesiologist operates a machine that controls the amount of gas a patient receives. While breathing the gas, the patient sleeps and feels no pain. The anesthesiologist must also monitor the patient's breathing and make sure that his or her general condition is satisfactory. The anesthetic gas, usually nitrous oxide, cyclopropane, or halothane, would kill the patient if used by itself over a long period, so oxygen must be given at the same time.

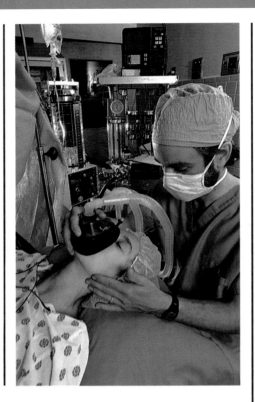

Numbing a Small Area

Special solutions are injected into the spinal canal for spinal anesthetics. Local anesthetics are injected into a nerve, or sprayed on the skin surface in the case of very short operations.

Treating Kidney Failure

There are two main treatments for kidney failure. One is *dialysis.* In hemodialysis, the person's blood is fed along tubes into an "artificial kidney machine" *(renal dialysis machine).* This filters out wastes and poisons, and then returns the blood to the body. A different form of dialysis is called peritoneal dialysis. A special fluid is injected into the abdomen, where it absorbs the wastes. It is drained away and replaced a few hours later. If kidney failure becomes long term, a better alternative is a kidney transplant. Such operations are highly successful and most patients can return to a normal live. However, as with the machines, there is always a shortage of suitable kidneys from donors.

Another Kind of Picture ▼

Ultrasonic waves travel through flesh and soft tissues and can be used by doctors in place of X rays to produce images of the internal organs and tissues of the human body. At low power, ultrasonic waves have no harmful effects on the body and are used for investigation and diagnosis. The so-called body scanner uses ultrasonics in the detection of tumors and blood clots. Ultrasonic scans are frequently given to pregnant women to make sure that the baby is growing at the right rate. The scan also checks for physical abnormalities, and whether there is more than one fetus in the womb. With modern equipment, doctors can actually obtain moving pictures of processes inside the body.

It's All in the Mind

Since the mind "lives" in the brain, illnesses of the mind are probably often brain disorders. Mental or psychiatric disorders such as schizophrenia, severe depression, and anxiety, probably have their basis in the brain's very complicated chemistry. However, researchers have a long way to go before they unravel the secret of how the brain works and how it goes wrong.

To Be Allergic

To have an allergy means to be affected by something that is harmless to most people. People can be allergic to all sorts of things, including certain foods. It is not clear why some people have allergies and others do not. Heredity seems to play a part in allergies. However, in many other cases of allergy no other member of the family has been allergic.

Powerful Drugs ▲

Depressants are drugs that slow the activity of the nervous system. They are used medically to relieve pain, bring on sleep, curb nervousness, or relieve anxiety. *Stimulants* speed up the nervous system. They include cocaine, which is used medically as a local anesthetic, and the amphetamines, which are used only occasionally to relieve mild depression. *Hallucinogens* cause hallucinations. They distort the sight and hearing. *Cannabis* in small doses may act as a mild depressant, or in large doses as a mild hallucinogen.

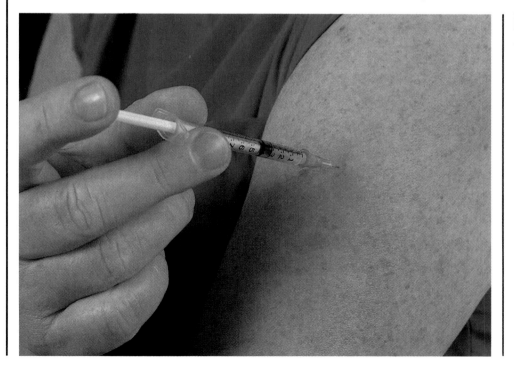

◄ Drugs Found in Nature

Some drugs have been prepared by extraction from organs of animals. Extracts of thyroid (a gland in the neck) were used in some thyroid disease. Insulin, which is used in the treatment of diabetes, was made from the pancreas of cows or pigs. Other drugs are extracted from minerals. They include mercury (for ointments), iodine (an antiseptic), and bromides (sedatives).

Functional Faucets

A faucet is a way of opening up a pipe to let water flow through. Turning the handle (or lifting a lever, depending on the kind of faucet you have) opens a valve that lets water pass by. The more you open the valve, the more water comes through. The water moves because of pressure inside the pipes. The pipes are filled with water, which is under pressure. When you open the valve, water comes through. Closing the valve stops the water from flowing.

The Wonder of Car Phones

Car phones work more like radios than actual telephones, since there are no wires connecting the phones to the telephone system. Each car phone is very much like an FM radio. It sends a signal that gets linked to the regular phone system so that calls can be made.

Cellular Phone News

Car phones are called "cellular phones" because the cellular radio network of car and portable phones splits each area into sections, or cells. As people drive from one cell to another, their calls are routed in special ways so that the phone call continues uninterrupted.

Talking on the Telephone

Telephones work by using electricity to increase the signal made by the sound of the human voice. Inside the handset (the thing you talk into and listen with) is a thin piece of plastic called a "diaphragm." When you speak into the phone, the diaphragm moves in and out. Each time it moves, tiny grains of carbon get pushed together or apart. This changes the flow of electricity inside the handset. When the electricity reaches another handset, it moves its diaphragm in exactly the same way, creating precisely the same sounds that were spoken into the phone.

Telephones of the Past

In the past, telephone messages got from one place to another by wire. This meant that all phones in the world were connected by telephone wiring systems. These systems were made up of hundreds of thousands of miles of cable running over land and even under the sea.

Telephone by Satellite

Today, the telephone system uses satellites to connect one phone to another. When you dial a number, the signal for your call goes to a telephone exchange. From there, it goes to a giant tower that sends it up to a communications satellite. The satellite then strengthens the signal and beams it to a receiving station near to where you are calling. The signal is then sent directly to the phone you want to call. Although it sounds very complicated, the whole process takes just seconds to complete.

◄ Smile and Say "Cheese"

To take a picture with a camera, you begin by pointing the camera at the person or scene you want to put on film. When you press the shutter button, light enters the camera for a fraction of a second to allow the image of the person or scene to enter the camera. The light coming into the camera acts on the light-sensitive film, putting the image onto the film. After it has been developed, the picture will show you exactly what you were pointing the camera at.

Making Cartoons Come Alive

It takes hundreds of hours of work to make today's animated cartoons, even though computers have made the job faster and easier. Cartoons are made by creating separate individual pictures for each step of an action. To show a character throwing a football, for example, cartoonists create dozens of pictures, each showing a separate step—how a football player lifts an arm, pulls it back, and then throws the ball through the air. These pictures are then photographed one after another and shown very quickly on the screen.

For Those Special Moments

The Polaroid-type camera uses a special film that can be developed inside the camera itself. This means that you can see your pictures just a few seconds after you take them. The film is coated with special chemicals that react inside the camera. When the film is taken from the camera, more chemicals react with the air and bring the finished picture onto the film.

Picture Perfect ▲

Automatic cameras have special cells that can measure the amount of light in the area around them. The camera is automatically adjusted so that it can take a picture with the proper amount of light. (Too much light makes the picture whitish; too little light makes it dark and unclear.)

Movies in Your Own Home ▲

A VCR is like a television set that has a tape recorder inside of it instead of a screen. The tape recorder can be used to record and play back programs that you would normally see on the TV screen. Or, it can be used to play back movies or other shows on tapes that you rent or buy in the store. The sights and sounds of your favorite movies and shows are turned into electronic signals, which are recorded on the tape as variations in a magnetic field. These are put onto the tape that is inside the video cassette. The VCR then reads the signals on the tape and transmits them back into pictures and sounds through a TV screen.

◄ Taking a Picture

Photographic film is coated with a thin layer (or layers) of light-sensitive *emulsion*, which consists of gelatin containing tiny crystals of chemicals called silver halides. When a picture is taken, the lens projects an image of the subject onto the film. In black-and-white film processing, the light that falls on the film causes some of the crystals in the emulsion to undergo a chemical change. When the film is soaked in a chemical solution called a *developer*, the crystals that have been affected by light change into specks of dark metallic silver and form a black *negative* image. The remaining crystals are unaffected and are washed away in a fixing bath. The developed film shows the darkest patches where most light has fallen, lighter patches where less light has fallen, and is quite transparent where no light has fallen. It is called a negative because it reverses the light and shade of the subject.

Lifelike Color Film

Color photography works on a similar principle, but the film has three individual layers of emulsion (sensitive to red, green, or blue). A silver image is formed in each layer that corresponds to the three colors of the original scene. This image is then made visible in the development process, which creates red, green, and blue areas in the film instead of black ones.

Film Editing ►

An editor or team of editors receives all of the parts of a film—sometimes in many pieces. The parts are then put together, taken apart, and reassembled until the editor and the director are satisfied. If a particular scene is too long, the editor can splice or cut out any number of frames to shorten the movie or arrange the frames in a different order. For this reason, film editors are really artists in their own right. They can remove the boring, poor scenes to make a film fast-moving and exciting, or they can change the whole way a story is told. As you might expect, it takes a crew of film editors up to six months to edit a major film.

◄ A Simple Music Machine

A music box contains tiny machinery that consists of a spring, a metal comb with teeth tuned to different notes, and a barrel studded with pins. When the wound-up spring is released, the barrel revolves and its pins strike the teeth of the comb, thus producing the tune.

Chiming and Ringing

Bells can be spherical or egg-shaped, but the typical bell most people know is the church bell, designed to be heard a long way away. There are two ways of sounding church bells—by chiming or by ringing. Chiming is a gentle method in which a wheel from below moves just enough for the clapper to hit the side of the bell. Ringing is a vigorous method in which the bell is swung full circle, starting from an upside-down position.

◄ A Traditional Instrument

Bagpipes consist of a bag, traditionally made from the skin of a goat or other animal, to which a set of pipes is attached. The bag is kept full of air, which is usually blown through the blowpipe from the mouth of the player, and is held under the left arm. Other pipes of various sizes are fixed in the bag, which when squeezed by the player's arm allows air to pass continuously to the pipes, causing them to make a sound. The sound is produced by the vibration of a reed as in a clarinet or oboe.

Making a Church Bell

The process of making a church bell is unique. After the dimensions of the bell have been worked out, a mold is made. This consists of a core of brick covered with a coating of loam or sand shaped to the inside of the bell around which the cope is constructed. The cope, also made of loam or sand, is shaped to the outside of the bell and fits over the core in such a way that a space is left between them. Molten bronze or bell metal is poured into the space at a temperature of 2000°F (1100°C). The cooling of the metal is carefully controlled to prevent the bell from cracking. After the bell has cooled (large bells may take up to two weeks), the mold is broken, and the rough casting of the bell is sand-blasted and polished. The bell-founder tunes the completed bell by revolving it and grinding away bits of metal from the inside.

Let's Make Music

The harmonica is a small wind instrument consisting of a series of reeds of different pitches fixed into metal plates and mounted on a long, flat, boxlike structure. To play a tune on a harmonica, the player puts his or her lips over holes in the top. By blowing or sucking, he or she forces air over the reeds and sets them vibrating freely from side to side.

Wonders of the Human Eye ▼

To make a movie, the camera actually takes hundreds of separate, slightly different photographs. When these pictures are projected onto a screen, each of them is seen for only a fraction of a second. But, instead of seeing hundreds of different pictures, we actually see one smooth motion. The key to this is something called "the persistence of visual movement." This is a wonder of the human eye. For example, if you are in a room and turn off the lights, you still see things even after you are completely in the dark. And, when you look at a string of pictures, your eyes see each one of them for a split second, even after the next one is in front of you. This makes the series of pictures look as if it is moving.

Sound and Action

In 1927, the first "talkies" appeared, and movies changed forever. To get sound to go with the film, moviemakers record the words of the actors when the action is being filmed. This is called *synchronous*, or sync, sound. Other sound effects—such as gunshots or footsteps—are recorded later.

Perfect Sound ▲

To make a digital recording, sounds are measured thousands of times per second. They are recorded as a series of pulses on tape. This allows the recording to be absolutely faithful to the original sound, even at the very loudest and softest points.

The Sounds of Stereo

Stereo works very much like the two ears of a person. If sound is recorded with one microphone, the result is very much like a person listening with one ear. To make stereo recordings, as many as 20 microphones are used, each connected to a separate amplifier. The sounds are then blended into two different *tracks,* containing the sounds for each speaker so that each ear hears a different sound. These are the upper and lower sections of the recording tape. When these are played back at the same time, the tape gives people the sense of distance, height, and movement they would hear in real life.

Laser Power

A CD (compact disc) player uses small plastic discs to reproduce sound better than any system yet devised. Sounds are placed on the disc using digital recording techniques. When you play the disc, a laser beam inside the CD player reads the information that has been placed on the disc. The information is then processed by the amplifier and speaker. Not only is the sound quality of a CD excellent, it is also more likely to stay that way than conventional records or tapes. That is because the information is read by beams of light, so there is no needle or magnetic head to wear down the recording.

It Sounds Like You're Right There

When Thomas Edison invented the phonograph back in the 1870s, he used needles to make his recordings as well as to play them back. Today, the needle, or "stylus," as it should be called, is used to play back records you buy in a store. The needle rides through the grooves on the record and reads the sounds that have been impressed on the plastic surface. This message is then sent to the amplifier and speakers to give you the sounds of the music. On stereo records, the needle actually moves in two different directions. By moving up and down and back and forth it gives you real-life sound.

Hearing Tunes

Radios use radio waves (a type of radiation found in nature) to send sounds from place to place. When your favorite disc jockey talks into a microphone, the sounds are picked up and turned into electrical current. This current is then turned into a radio wave and transmitted from an antenna. When you turn your radio to a particular station, it picks up all of the passing radio waves and filters out all of them except the one you have chosen. Your radio increases (amplifies) that wave and separates the sounds that the DJ spoke into the microphone. Those sounds are then sent to the loudspeaker so you can hear them.

Old-fashioned Typewriters ▲

The simplest typewriters have long "fingers," at the end of which are metal letters. Pressing a key moves the finger toward the paper. The letter then strikes an ink-soaked ribbon and leaves an ink impression of the letter on the paper. A lever lets you move the page down a line when you have reached the right-hand edge of the paper.

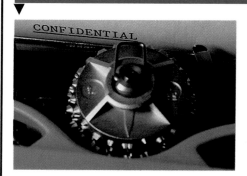

Typing Made Easy

Electric typewriters use electricity to print letters on paper. It takes a lot less effort to press the keys than on a conventional typewriter. And, you simply press a button to make the paper roll up another line.

State-of-the-Art Typewriters

Electronic typewriters use a spinning ball or wheel instead of the long "fingers" found on conventional typewriters. When you strike a key, an electronic signal is sent to the ball or wheel and it presses that letter against the ribbon. This leaves the mark of the letter on the paper. Because there are fewer moving parts, electronic typewriters are faster than conventional typewriters. They also break down less often.

Let There Be Light

An incandescent light bulb is made up of a thin strip of metal wire inside a bulb filled with nitrogen and other gases. Electricity is used to get the metal so hot that it glows and makes light. You can change the color of the light in several ways. You can paint the bulb a certain color (blue, red, green, and so on, just like the bulbs that you see on Christmas trees). Or, you can use different kinds of metal. Certain metals, for example, give off a yellowish light; others make a light that is closer to a pure white in color.

Correcting Mistakes ▲

In the 1960s, the self-correcting typewriter was invented. When you made a mistake, you back-spaced to that place and typed the wrong letters again over a thin ribbon of chalk or chemicals. This covered the mistake and made it disappear. Then you typed the correct letter in its place. Now, electronic typewriters keep your work in their memory. You simply watch a screen and make your corrections even before the letters are printed on the page.

By the Flip of a Switch▲

Getting electricity to a bulb when you need it is done through a light switch. When the light switch is in the "off" position, there is a gap in the wires through which electricity flows. Turning the switch "on" closes the gap and lets the electricity flow through. Some switches allow different amounts of electricity to go through, making the lights brighter or dimmer.

Bridging the Gap ▲

There are several different kinds of bridges. The simplest kind is made by stretching a tree or piece of lumber between two points—across a river, a stream, or over a ditch. Other bridges use an arch to give strength to the part of the bridge that has nothing underneath it. The most complicated bridges are suspension bridges. These use wires and cables to hang the bridge over a long stretch of water or space. The cables hold the bridge's roadway in place and keep it from falling down.

More Lights

Fluorescent lights, which are usually tubular in shape, work by heating gases rather than a metal strip. The inside of the tube is coated with a special powder that contains phosphorus. It also contains mercury vapor, which produces ultraviolet rays when an electric current passes through it. The powder glows when it is struck by the ultraviolet rays from the electric discharge. The light that fluorescent lights produce is more like daylight than the light produced by incandescent bulbs.

Romantic Water Wheels ▲

Water wheels were one of the earliest—and most important—machines. The wheel was set up near a stream of flowing water with buckets hooked up to it. The buckets fill with water at the top of the wheel. The water spills out as each bucket nears the bottom. Because the heavy buckets were all on one side of the wheel, the weight kept the wheel turning around and around. The wheel was attached to a large pole, or shaft. This could be used to turn other wheels or giant stones for grinding flour.

Bridges that Move ▼

Drawbridges are used wherever tall boats cannot pass under a bridge. The most common of them is called a swing bridge. The roadway of a swing bridge is mounted on a giant turntable. When a boat is to come through, the turntable twists the road out of the way. The drawbridge that is the most fun to watch is called a jackknife bridge. It has two sections that can tilt up on end. When a boat needs to come through, giant jacks (a lot like the ones you use to lift up your car when you have to change a flat tire) lift the sections into the air. When the boat has passed, the jacks lower the roadway back down again.

Do You Know the Combination?

A combination lock has one or more rings threaded onto a spindle. When the rings are turned to a particular letter or number, slots inside the rings fall into line. This allows the spindle to be drawn out and the lock to be opened.

Up and Down the Escalator

An escalator is a set of steps that has been attached to a moving chain. At the top and bottom of the chain are wheels with metal or plastic teeth. An electric motor turns the wheel at the top of the stairs. When the motor is turned on, it pulls the steps upward and, when they reach the top, sends them back down again underneath. The steps are made so that they can bend and fold as they travel down along the underside of the escalator.

Locking Up

A lock is a bolt that holds a door and door frame together. When a door is locked, pins inside keep it from being opened. Most of today's locks are based on a design made by Linus Yale, back in 1848. The Yale lock has five different pins that are pressed into a cylinder by springs. These pins keep the cylinder from turning and the door from being opened. When the key is put into the lock, it pushes the pins to the right height and allows the cylinder to turn.

Making Fire

Fire can be made in several ways. In Alaska, for example, some Indian peoples rub sulfur over two stones and then strike them together. This age-old method can be very effective, especially if the stones are flint, which sparks very easily. In China and India, people often strike a piece of broken pottery against a bamboo stick. Once a spark is made, the fire slowly builds up. The ancient Greeks and Romans used glass to make their fires. They used what was called a "burning glass" to focus the rays of the sun on some dry grass or wood. In the early days of the United States, people often carried a tinderbox. This was a metal box with a flint and steel. People struck the steel against the flint until sparks fell into the cotton placed inside the box. The burning cotton was used to light larger fires.

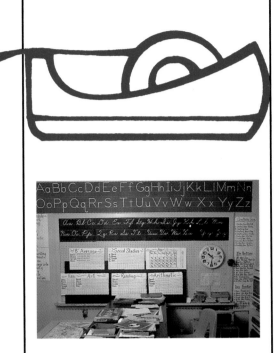

Taping It Together

Scotch tape is actually a brand name for just one of the many hundreds of different clear tapes that you can buy in the store. It works because a chemical called an "adhesive" is placed on one side of the tape. This chemical makes a bond with another surface that is so strong that you cannot simply lift the tape off. Many different ingredients can be used to make adhesives, including animal bones, flour, and even plastics.

Zipping It Up

A zipper is made of two strips of metal or plastic teeth that have been sewn to the sides of an opening. (It can be an opening in a shirt, some pants, or even a suitcase.) A sliding hook is attached to the strips. To close the opening, you link the two edges together and pull the hook towards the top of the zipper. The hook pulls the edges together and locks each of the teeth to the one behind it. When you open the zipper, the hook moves downward and separates the teeth.

Learning Your ABCs ▲

The letters of the alphabet are really signs, or symbols, that stand for different sounds. As we see each letter in a word, we silently say each sound to ourselves. When we put all those sounds together, we can say the word in front of us. It took many thousands of years for people to create an alphabet. And, in fact, the very first kinds of writing used pictures to show what the writer was describing. But, since pictures can be hard to draw—and it is almost impossible to illustrate ideas—people gradually shifted to an alphabet using letters. The English alphabet uses 26 letters, although other alphabets have more or fewer letters.

The Engine Makes It Run ▲

Cars need engines of one kind or another in order to work. Internal combustion engines that burn gasoline are the most common kind of automobile engine. Other car engines have included electrical and steam motors. The car's engine provides the energy to make the car move. Its transmission joins the engine to the wheels, which actually move the car.

Cleaning Without Water

Modern dry cleaning usually uses petroleum or synthetic solvents. The petroleum type can be used in an open machine like a washing machine, but synthetic solvents evaporate quickly in the air and must be used in closed, airtight machines. Items for cleaning are sorted according to their fiber and color. The process is similar to washing and rinsing, except that the solvent is used instead of water. Since the solvent evaporates quickly, cleaning by this method is "dry," or without water. After cleaning, garments are pressed with steam to return them to their proper shape.

Using a Die

A die is a type of tool that is used in shaping, casting, cutting, or trimming materials such as metals, plastics, or fabrics. The body parts on automobiles are formed in dies built so that the top and bottom parts of the die are of the same shape. There is only enough space between the upper and lower sections of the die for a flat piece of metal. When the metal is placed in the die and pressure is applied, the sheet immediately takes the form of the die. After the part is formed, it is removed and trimmed in a trimming or blanking die. This type of die is like a pair of scissors or paper cutter. One blade passes another so that it will cut the metal instead of forming it.

Water purification plant

Technicians evaluate the water at this purification plant

Purifying a Liquid

Distillation is the process that purifies any liquid. An apparatus for distilling is usually called a still and has three main parts: the boiler, the cooler or condenser, and the receiver to catch the condensed liquid or "distillate."

The largest stills are those used on land to obtain fresh water for drinking from seawater. Fresh water is produced by stills in many places where rainfall is low. A distillation plant on an artificial island near Los Angeles is designed to produce 65 million gallons (250 million liters) a day, using nuclear reactors to supply the heat needed to change the water into steam.

Lots of Colored Images

A kaleidoscope is an instrument that shows regular patterns when you look into it. It is a tube about 1 foot (30 cm) long, with two or three plain mirrors running the length of the tube and fastened at a 60–degree angle. One end of the tube has a peephole and the other is closed with a piece of non-transparent glass. On this are several loose fragments of colored glass covered with a piece of clear glass. When you look into the peephole, several images of each fragment are seen, because the image formed in one mirror is also reflected by the other and so on. All the images together form a regular pattern that can be completely changed by shaking the tube so as to move the glass fragments to new positions.

Preserving Food the Dry Way

Freeze-drying is a form of food preservation that rapidly freezes the food in a high vacuum. Under these conditions, the ice crystals sublime and the water vapor is removed to leave the food dehydrated and in the best condition for later rehydration (addition of water) when it is to be eaten.

A Roof for Each Purpose ▲

The roof of a building largely reflects the climate of the place in which the building stands. In dry countries, roofs are flat and can be used as an outdoor room when the sun is not too hot. In an area where it often rains, the roof usually slopes so that the water can run off it. Where there are heavy snowfalls, the roof slopes steeply so that the snow will slide off and not build up into a thick layer.

Better Than Soap ◄

Non-soap detergents do not depend on natural edible fats as a basic raw material, since they are made from petroleum and the by-products of coal. They can be specially made to lather well in hard or salt water, to rinse easily from fabrics or from dishes, and in fact to perform many tasks for which soap is not satisfactory.

Switching Gears

A car's clutch, when pressed to the floor, disconnects the engine from the transmission. This allows you to change gears so that you can move faster or have more pulling power. The gears allow the car to travel slowly even though the engine is running very quickly.

The Ease of Automatic Transmission ▲

Automatic transmissions contain fluid that allows the car to change gears by itself, depending on how fast the engine is working and how fast the car is going.

How Fast Are You Going? ▲

A car's speedometer is connected to a set of gears inside its transmission. When the car starts moving, these gears turn the shaft that connects the speedometer to the transmission. This shaft turns a magnet that controls the speedometer's needle. As it turns, it points to the speed at which the car is traveling.

Mirror, Mirror on the Wall ▶

Mirrors have been around since the days of the ancient Egyptians, and all mirrors work in basically the same way. A mirror is a polished surface, usually metal or even a piece of glass with a special coating put on it. When light strikes this surface, it bounces off at exactly the same angle at which it first struck the surface—it reflects exactly the same image that is striking it.

Under a Microscope

Microscopes use a hollow tube and different lenses to magnify, or make larger, things that people want to see. As light passes through the lower lens, it is concentrated by a group of lenses. You can then use the lenses just as you would a telescope. The difference is that a microscope has one set of lenses that magnifies the image produced by another set of lenses.

Telescopic Vision

The simplest telescope is called a "refracting" telescope. It is made up of a hollow tube and two different-sized lenses. The larger lens, called the objective lens, gathers light rays coming from things far away. The small lens at the other end of the tube then magnifies, or makes larger, the image seen in the objective lens. A third lens in the center inverts the image— otherwise it would be upside down.

A Mirror Image

There is one slight difference between an original image and a mirror image. A person looking at himself or herself in the mirror sees an opposite picture in which the left and right sides have been turned around. That means that your left eye is looking at the mirror image's right eye; your right eye is looking at the left eye of the image in the mirror.

Blending into the Scenery

Camouflage is a way to disguise or hide things in nature as well as in the armies of the world. In nature, many animals have special colorings that help them hide from those creatures that can harm them. Soldiers have used camouflage for hundreds of years. Today's soldiers wear camouflage suits made of blotches of green, black, and brown colors. This makes the clothing look like part of the jungle or forest.

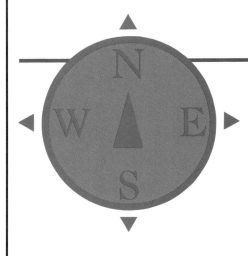

A Compass Points North

A magnetic compass is made of a magnetized needle that can turn freely—on a floating piece of cork, a sharp point, or anything similar to it. It points north because magnets attract one another. Our earth behaves as if there were a giant magnet at its center, and it attracts the tiny magnet used in a compass. The north that the compass points to, though, is not the geographic north of the North Pole. Instead, it points to what is called "magnetic north," a point about 1,000 miles (1,600 km) away from the North Pole.

Cutting a Diamond to Shape ▲

Diamonds are found in nature. But, without a lot of careful, hard work, they are really nothing much to look at. Once a diamond has been found, it is taken to a diamond-cutting center, where it is sorted according to color, size, and clarity. Then, it is cut into the best possible shape. This is a complicated job that can only be done by a skilled, experienced worker.

Powerful Lasers ▼

The laser is a machine that makes a bright light of a single wavelength and color. Unlike regular light, which goes out in all directions, the laser gives a very narrow beam of highly concentrated light. The way these beams are created and the kind of light they produce give lasers great power to light things up and even to produce heat and energy.

Computerized Typing ▲

A word processor is a computer-type machine that takes the place of a typewriter. When you type the words you want on a keyboard, electronic signals are sent to the computer "brain" where letters are formed and projected onto a video screen. Because these are electronic signals, you can change, erase, or move them using other electronic signals. Then, when you are ready to make a printed copy of your work, you simply tell the "brain" to send the work to the printer.

Lasers and Music

Lasers can "read" records or discs because there is a glass tube filled with special gases that is placed between two mirrors inside the laser machine. When electricity passes through the tube, a deep red beam of light is produced. This can be used to "read" or decode electronic signals placed on a plastic disc. The signals are then sent to be increased and broadcast through speakers.

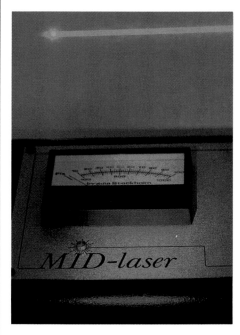

The Mind of a Computer

Computers all work pretty much the same way. Electronic signals (from words, numbers, symbols, etc.) come into an input unit. These signals are passed to a memory unit, where they are stored. A central processing unit then carries out what has to be done—adding or subtracting, putting words on a screen, or even moving a ball around in a computer game. The new signals are then sent to an output unit, which is usually a television-type screen or a printer. Because everything happens electronically, all of this takes only a fraction of a second to carry out.

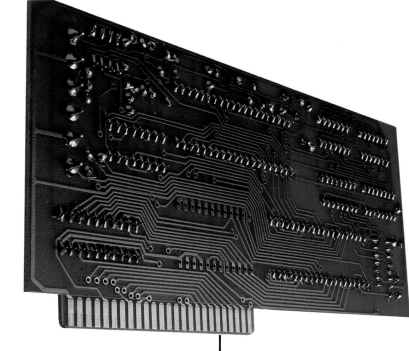

Supermarket Laser Scanners

Today's supermarkets often use lasers to "read" the prices on the things you buy. Each item is marked with a special code. (You can see it. It's the block of black lines on the outside of the package.) When you buy something, the clerk in the store passes the object over the laser scanner. The laser identifies the lines and their widths, and a small computer tells the cash register what the item is and how much it costs. That's why your sales slip not only tells you how much you spent, but what you bought and what it cost.

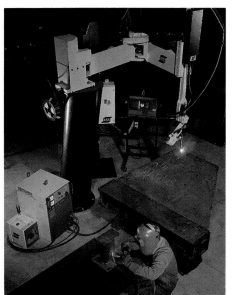

◄Working Robots

Computerized robots are computers with machines attached to them. These machines can move things, rivet or weld objects together, or even inspect the quality of things that have been made. The computer "brains" are given programs telling them what to do. There also are special sensors that let the "brain" know about things around it—other machines coming near, temperature changes, and so on. None of these machines can actually think, and they need people to write the programs that they carry out. But, they often can do jobs even better than people, as well as take on jobs that people could never do themselves.

Making a Computer Work

A computer program is a set of instructions telling a computer what to do. The program may tell it to "input," to "print," or even to let one symbol stand for another in a code. Writing a program is a matter of knowing the right language and getting the directions to the computer in exactly the right order.

31